Ortelius, Abraham. *Islandia* in *Theatrvm Orbis Terrarvm*, 1587, based on original map accredited to Guðbrandur Þorláksson, bishop at Hólar in Skagafjörður, Northern Iceland. In: Grétarsson, Reynir Finndal. *Maps of Iceland: Antique Maps of Iceland, 1482-1850*. Reykjavík:2018, Crymogea 2018-12-17.

GUÐRÍÐUR'S SAGA
COLORING BOOK

ICELANDIC ROOTS

GUÐRÍÐUR'S SAGA

COLORING BOOK

WRITTEN BY
BRYNDÍS VÍGLUNSDÓTTIR

ILLUSTRATED BY
GAY STRANDEMO

ICELANDIC ROOTS

Guðríður's Saga Coloring Book
Copyright © 2022 by Bryndís Viglundsdottír

All rights reserved. No part of this publication may be reproduced, distributed, or transmitted in any form or by any means, including photocopying, recording, or other electronic or mechanical methods, without the prior written permission of the author, except in the case of brief quotations embodied in critical reviews and certain other non-commercial uses permitted by copyright law.

Tellwell Talent
www.tellwell.ca

ISBN
978-0-2288-7244-3 (Paperback)

Dedication

For all children who ask questions

How to Use This Book

On every page, across from every drawing there will be questions to help you come up with things to draw so you can share this story.
Take a picture of your drawings with your phone or make a
copy and send it to icelandicroots.com to share them with everyone!

Introduction

Just before the year 1000 CE, about twenty years before Leif Erikson sailed to America, a girl who would become the most traveled woman of the Viking Age was born at the farm Laugarbrekka on Snæfellsnes in Iceland. It was a beautiful place where she went fishing and helped herd the sheep.

Erik the Red, Leif's father, had emigrated to Greenland, claiming it was easier to make a living there than in Iceland. Convinced, Guðríður's parents decided to leave Iceland and settle in Greenland. Despite rough sailing with high winds, fog and ice on the sea, the family luckily reached the settlement in Greenland safely.

When Guðríður was a young woman, a seafarer and merchant, Þorfinnur karlsefni sailed to Greenland. He had heard about land in the west called Vínland the Good. Guðríður and Þorfinnur married and became determined to find that land. They sailed to Vínland and found it much to their liking.

They stayed three years in Vínland and during that time, Snorri, their son was born— the first European child known to have been born in North America. After three years spent in Vínland, the family moved to Skagafjörður, Iceland, and lived on a farm named Glaumbær, which now is the site of an Icelandic National Museum.

In this story, Guðríður's young grandson Þorgeir asks his grandmother about her extraordinary life. We hope all children will enjoy hearing Guðríður's adventures!

What is your favorite animal? Please draw a picture!

What animals do you see where you live?
Please, draw some of them!

What would you bring to your amma (grandmother)?

Can you draw a picture of you or someone else on a sunny day?

Can you draw a picture of a place that is frosty and cold?

Can you draw a picture of animals you see every day?

Can you draw a picture of yourself running?

Here is a picture of Guðríður and Þorfinnur.
Can you draw a picture of your family?

Can you draw some thing that is important to you?

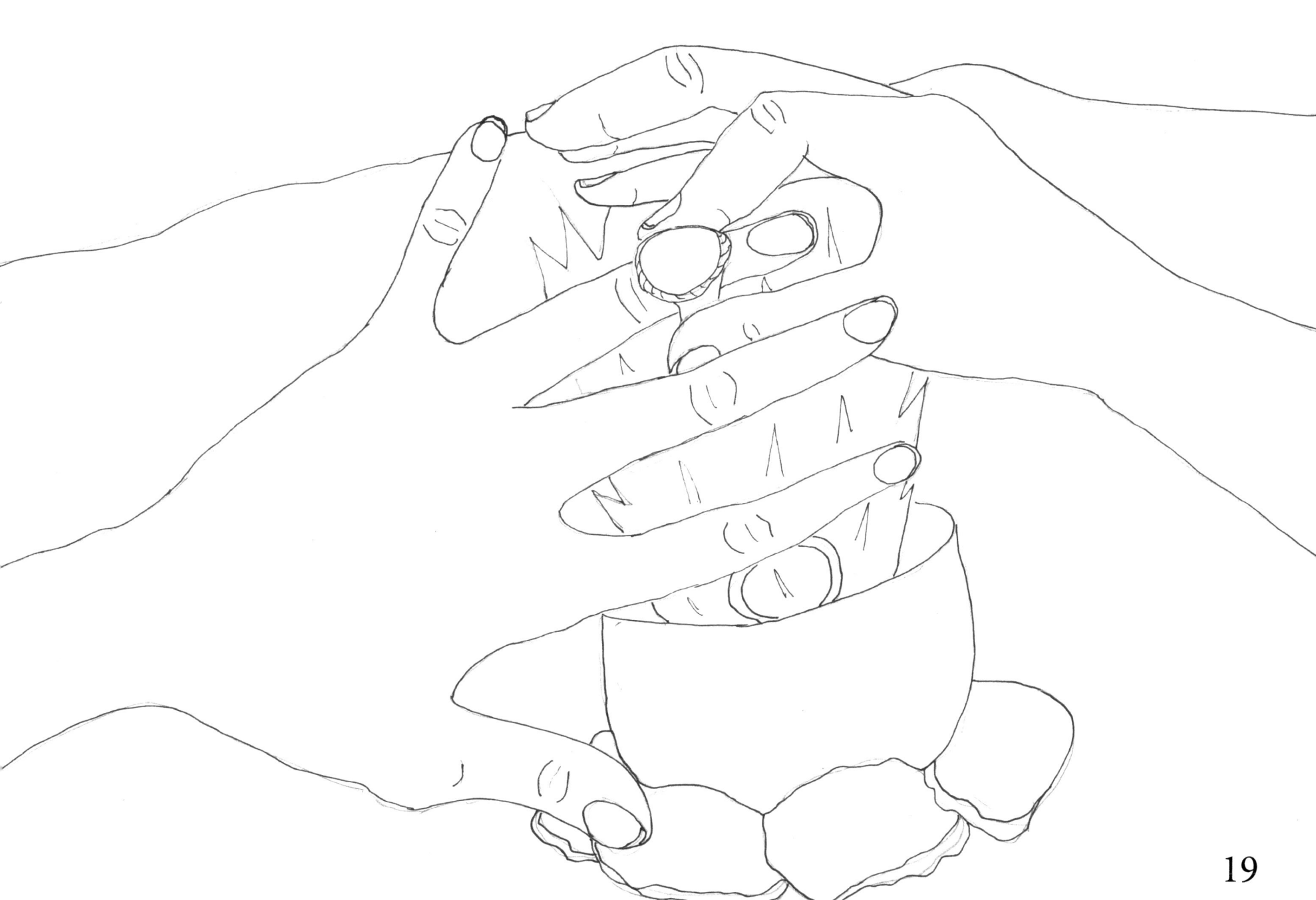

What do you think Guðríður took with her sailing from Greenland to Vínland? Please, draw them.

How do you think Guðríður and Snorri looked?
A picture by you would be nice.

Please, draw a picture of your friend.

Have you ever been surprised by something?
Please, draw what happened.

Guðríður walked to Rome, around the year 1000. She saw many things. Can you draw what she might have seen on her travels?

Did you know that people in Iceland once lived in turf houses, made of grass and packed dirt?
Please, draw a picture of the place where you live!

www.ingramcontent.com/pod-product-compliance
Lightning Source LLC
LaVergne TN
LVHW071732060526
838200LV00031B/480